G000275350

STYLE IN MY DNA

LORNA HOLDER

▲ Mid-1970s London – Lorna Holder. Photographer Errol Holder © Tuareg Productions

First published 2018 by Tuareg Productions Ltd

All enquiries should be addressed to
Tuareg Productions Ltd, c/o Citycas Ltd,
Suite 540, Fifth Floor, Linen Hall,
162-168 Regent Street, London W1B 5TP

www.tuaregproductions.com

Telephone: 0207 692 2711

ISBN 978-0-9549907 -8-7

Fashion Illustrations by Warren Holder
Print & Design: CPUK Print Publishing Ltd.
Designer: Lee Zaninetti
Editor: Angela Baynham

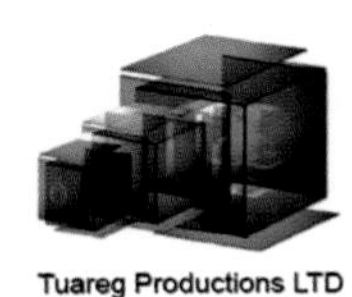

LORNA HOLDER: Born in Jamaica but raised in Nottingham (UK), Lorna has more than 35 years' experience at executive level in the fashion and retail industries, cultural events, visual and performing arts. She graduated in 1975 from Trent University, Nottingham, with BA Honours in Fashion & Textiles. She went on to work in the Middle East, New York and London in fashion and retail. She worked as a designer for the Birmingham-based design company House of Lerose and was head of fashion during the 1970s and 1980s for Davies & Fields, one of Britain's largest dress manufacturing companies.

Lorna was the executive producer for the first Black Film & Television Awards held in 2002 at Grosvenor House, Park Lane. She has delivered six Heritage Lottery Fund productions (2004-2015), based on research and oral histories from Caribbean people and other communities in Britain and has also collaborated with the V&A, British Museum, Rich Mix, BFI, Theatre Royal Nottingham and London Metropolitan Archives.

Lorna wrote, produced and directed the *Living Under One Roof* stage play (2003-2007). She also wrote and produced *The Ones We Left Behind* (2006) and *Moving Out* (2007) theatre productions and produced and directed the *Building Bridges* (2008) documentary. She curated the *Living Under One Roof* (2009) exhibition – Bamako Encounters, African Photography Biennia. She produced and directed the *Hanging Out* documentary (2012) and curated the *Hanging Out* exhibition at the V&A. She produced and curated the Jamaica Hidden Histories project (2012-2015).

Lorna's business archives have been acquired by the London Metropolitan Archives and her British Caribbean photographic collection by Mary Evans Picture Agency. Lorna is a member of the Board of Governors for Nottingham Trent University, New Art Exchange in Nottingham, and is the managing director for Full Spectrum and Tuareg Productions.

Lorna has been married for 41 years and has three grown-up sons.

CONTENTS

FOREWORD

In 1959, like many Caribbean children of the time, Lorna Holder came to England to join her mother, who had left Jamaica two years earlier in search of a better life for herself and her family. Photographs, letters and parcels sent back to Jamaica had helped to sustain the bond between mother, daughter and other cherished family members left behind.

Growing up in Nottingham, Lorna's first exposure to Caribbean fashion in the UK was obtained through the art of seeing. While magazines and cinema would dictate fashion trends to the British masses, few recorded the evolution of style within Britain's burgeoning Caribbean community. Desperate to ensure that the community's development and consequent contribution to British fashion culture did not go unpreserved, Lorna documented the changes within her community at a time when few outlets would. Although unbeknownst to her at the time, as Lorna chronicled the ever-changing tide of Caribbean fashion within the UK, she was slowly planting the creative seeds which would one day lead to a career within the fashion industry and to the photographs you see within this book.

The 1950s and '60s would see the invention of 'the teenager'. James Dean's portrayal of Jim Stark in *Rebel Without a Cause* would see the teenage character tear away from the conformist standards set by his parents. In the UK, Twiggy's short hair and miniskirts again sent a clear message to the generations that came before them, that message being, "We are not you".

In the 1970s, for the first time in history teenagers of Caribbean descent living in the UK would declare themselves 'Black-British' and assert precisely what that meant to them. For Lorna, this time of significant change would see the young artist take fashion seriously and gain control over her life's narrative.

Her life of self-determination and perseverance thwarted every force that attempted to limit her ambitions. Lorna had not left Jamaica and travelled 5,000 miles across the world to be brought down by negativity, nor would she let it define her.

Lorna's continuous documentation of fashion trends from the 1940s to the present day takes us on a journey through time to observe the evolution of fashion within the British Caribbean community. Through the eyes of a fashion designer, see the many ways in which Lorna's Caribbean contemporaries demonstrated confidence, personality and style, which still to this day influences the fashion landscape.

It gives me great pleasure to present *Style in my DNA*. To bear witness to the fundamental ways Caribbean culture and fashion have shaped the UK and beyond is to ensure that the significant contributions made throughout the years will never be forgotten.

Enjoy,

Miles Holder
Editor-In-Chief - FAULT Magazine

70 YEARS OF BRITISH CARIBBEAN FASHION

The archive photographs we so often see of Caribbean men arriving on *SS Empire Windrush* in June 1948 were, and still are, powerful, captivating images of a time in our history when the clothes we wore defined who we were, our culture and our identity.

Fashion designers, artist and filmmakers have always drawn from various sources for inspiration. I am no different; my inspirations and references come from film, photography and travel. As a women's wear fashion designer (1975-2003) preparing a collection based on 1940s black American glamour, the film *Carmen Jones* with Dorothy Dandridge and Harry Belafonte would immediately come to mind. The British film *A Kind of Loving* with Alan Bates and June Ritchie reflects, through its choice of fashion, the everyday lives of working-class people in 1960s Britain. We should not forget the eclectic 1970s, with Jimmy Cliff's film *The Harder They Come* presenting urban Jamaican culture through its fashion and music.

Archive photographs, record covers and fashion catalogues were also excellent sources of information, allowing me to examine closely the cut of a garment, hemline, fabric texture, colour and the overall fashion statement. Travelling to various parts of the world, meeting interesting and diverse people, has always boosted my creativity. This information would give me all I needed to create that winning number.

THE LATE 1940s

More than 400 men arrived on *SS Empire Windrush* in June 1948 at Tilbury Docks, mostly from Jamaica, others from Trinidad and Barbados. Some were ex-servicemen who had fought for Britain in the Second World War. Many were professionals with a variety of skills. Sadly, unemployment was high throughout the Caribbean, and many looked towards Britain for a better life. The majority came with the intention to work, and they helped rebuild Britain after the War.

I do believe we are all inspired by what we see and experience, and I cannot help feeling it was the films of the late 1940s that inspired the wardrobe of the first Windrush generation. Cinema was a massive force in the Caribbean Islands. In fact, every major town in the urban and rural areas of Jamaica had cinemas (often called theatres) in the 1940s. The cinema was a place of pure escapism. The men who arrived at Tilbury Docks did not come in their ordinary working clothes, but in well-tailored, well-coordinated, American-inspired, 1940s suits, shirts, colourful silk ties, brightly coloured knitted sweaters, Trilby hats and two-tone shoes. Back in the Caribbean, as well as in films they would have seen the latest look in black American fashion magazines and catalogues, and had their garments made by the numerous tailors, shoemakers and dressmakers on the islands. Many had clothes, fabric lengths, shoes and hats sent to them from relatives in America.

The men would have bought readymade clothes such as shirts and ties, and the zoot suits. The zoot suit, inspired by the black American musicians of the early 1940s, comprised of wide-legged trousers, high waisted with braces, worn with a very long jacket with broad, padded shoulders, wide collar and lapels. We must not forget that throughout the Caribbean there were many Jewish and Syrian-owned department stores and dress shops, as well as the well-known chain Bata Shoes supplying their needs. As a result, the style of the Caribbean men who arrived at Tilbury Docks was not mainstream British. The Second World War had not long finished, and the overall look for British men was the navy or grey pinstripe utility suit.

Although not well documented, we had in Britain before, during and after the Second World War many Caribbean women working in the hospitals and the armed forces. Working women's clothes of the late 1940s were still affected by wartime rationing, and fashion was based on the utility shape seen throughout the War. The utility style was a practical, tailored, slimline shape that required less fabric.

A typical outfit for women was the two-piece woollen tailored suit. The jacket was hip length with padded shoulders. It had a narrow collar, two or three buttons at the front, small welt or patch pockets and with a slightly nipped-in waist. The jacket was worn with a simple knee-length, A-line or straight pencil skirt or trousers. The typical everyday dress had padded shoulders, small collar, button front, a fitted waist and with two front pleats or simple A-line, knee-length skirt.

During the War, women covered their heads with protective head wears. After the War, they wore small, neat felt hats, headscarves and turbans. By the late 1940s, the 'New Look' (1947) began to replace the wartime utility fashions. Younger women particularly adopted the softer feminine look. Dresses were made without pads and had neat accentuated waistlines with fuller, longer skirts.

The delight we first saw in the faces of the Windrush men on arrival in Britain did not last. Reality set in when many Caribbean people found it hard to settle in Britain. The signs in windows that read 'No Blacks, No Dogs, No Irish', and other rejections from the host community were painful to bear. The mood of the country was still very bleak and unsure. Some returned home to the Caribbean, others decided to stick it out for five years, but many chose to stay.

▲ 1948 Jamaicans on board the *Empire Windrush*. © Illustrated London News Ltd/Mary Evans Picture Library
▶ 1940s Caribbean. © Margaret Andrews family archives

▲ Late 1940s Caribbean. © Margaret Andrews family archives
◄ Late 1940s Jamaica – bride and groom. © Beverly Provost OBE

THE 1950s

Many Caribbean women joined their husbands and partners in Britain in the early 1950s. Some had to take desperate measures, leaving their children behind and working all hours to make ends meet. Many families often slept in one room, cooking on the stair landings in poor, run-down houses, especially in the larger cities.

There was unrest within Caribbean households in Britain, many feeling they had made a huge mistake in leaving their homelands. The Government and business leaders wanted to demonstrate to the country the perfect domesticated and happy home. They built new social houses, produced household appliances and gadgets such as washing machines, fridges, televisions, morning tea makers and comfortable clothes. Sadly, this did not answer nor address the social and economic needs of the new migrant population.

In saying that, I did have family members in Nottingham who made the most of living in Britain. Many were used to travelling to different countries to live and work. They would have worked in Florida on the farms in the 1940s, and around other Caribbean Islands and experienced different social and cultural behaviours.

Most of the people my family knew in Nottingham came to Britain by aeroplane and were from the same district or town in Jamaica. They would always share information and news from back home. They had formed supportive networks, where elders such as my grandfather would help newcomers in dealing with the bank and mortgage applications. Women would help look after each other's children, visit the sick and elderly, and share the content of the many parcels they received from Jamaica: familiar dried bush teas, dried peas, spices, cocoa, fruitcakes and sweets.

My grandfather was an ex-Jamaican policeman, now a carpenter and a Deacon at the Wood Borough Road Baptist Church. He had purchased a house on Colville Street in Nottingham in 1957. The house had five bedrooms, two reception rooms, dining room, utility room, attic, cellar and a big garden. In this house my family felt sheltered from the rejections that so many Caribbean people encountered in coming to the Motherland.

British colonisation helped to produce a culture of formality in dress and behaviour in the Caribbean, especially after the War. Some people, like my great-grandmother, Sarah Jane, upheld it dearly; others looked towards America for a certain looseness in conduct and dress. I now understand why so many of the men in the archive photographs and films came off the *Empire Windrush* full of optimism and American swagger. After the Second World War, American culture did help to raise our self-esteem, both in the Caribbean and in Britain.

I remember in the mid-1950s in St Thomas, Jamaica, the excitement within my family in receiving a parcel that arrived with clothing from my great-aunt in New York. The garments were always more exciting than the ones sent from the UK. In fact, I remember my mother receiving a white, silk, ruffled-collar, organza blouse, with small pearl buttons. I have this blouse and still wear it with pride today. It was also an exciting time for my young uncles, receiving the latest fashion such as Hawaiian shirts, cotton bomber jackets inspired by Marlon Brando in *A Streetcar Named Desire* (1951), and dark blue denim jeans worn by Elvis Presley in *Jailhouse Rock* (1957).

My very tenacious, yet stylish, great-grandmother was my first source of inspiration. She and my maroon great-grandfather had left Jamaica in early 1900. They lived and worked in Panama, Costa Rica and Cuba, had children, then finally returned to Jamaica in the 1930s. My mother had left me in their care from 1957 to 1959 when she went to England. Not a day went by in St Thomas when people were not packing up, waving goodbye, crying as they were leaving loved ones behind. When a plane took off overhead, my great-grandmother would say, "there goes another one off to de Motherland".

I believe that my great-grandmother more than anyone had a significant impact on my attention to detail and my steel-like determination. I remember her wearing the dress in the picture. A mid-grey, linen, pleated dress, with a distinct 1940s button feature, worn with a cream belt and brown peep-toe shoes for our photo session in Spanish Town. She saw it as her responsibility to take all her grand- and great-grandchildren left in her care to have their pictures taken to send to their parents in England or America.

A local dressmaker made the little white organza dress I wore in the picture; we had many dressmakers in the district. My great-grandmother insisted I held a white cotton handkerchief in one hand, just like her, and to stand straight and look serious. On returning home, my outfit would be taken off in a flash and put away, and I changed into our judging clothes (house clothes). The same would apply to school uniform. On no account were we to be seen playing in our school uniform. It was a very tight ask of a five year old, but in time I got used to it and perhaps carried some of those disciplines many years later with my three sons.

In November 1959, aged seven, it was my turn to say farewell to my great-grandparents and to join my mother in England. I flew with my Uncle Horace, who was 19, from Palisadoes Airport (now Norman Manley International Airport) stopping off in New York. As the plane approached Manhattan Island, I found the dark sky illuminated by splashes of bright fluorescent lights so captivating. The plane landed at Gatwick Airport, where my mother collected me, and we drove to my grandfather's house in Nottingham. My mother was now married to my stepfather George Harris, and I had a baby brother, Kenneth.

In Britain, during the Second World War, while the men were away the women had the responsibility of doing the labour-intensive work. After the War, there was a conscious drive to entice women back into the home, evident in the designing and manufacturing of new household appliances, fashion and lifestyle products. The development of synthetic fabrics – nylon, polyester and acetate – was a huge breakthrough to support a modern lifestyle. These were in high demand due to their crease-resistant quality and easy washing.

The fashion of the early 1950s saw feminine, fitted-waist dresses, sometimes worn with crinolines in textured fabrics such as brocade, cotton stripes, floral and checks. Little knitted cardigans or short, waist-length jackets were worn with full-circled skirts with appliqués and pillar-box hats, especially for special occasions. Towards the late 1950s, semi-fitted, softly tailored suits were in vogue. I remember, back in Jamaica, seeing this picture (see page 29) of my mother wearing one of these suits when she first arrived in Nottingham in 1957. Caribbean families in Britain used photographs as a means of communicating with their loved ones left behind.

The films of the 1950s played a large part in determining how men dressed. Cinema was one of the few places young Caribbean men would go for entertainment in Britain. They would have witnessed the changes in attitudes and the emergence of American youth culture through the films of Marlon Brando, such as *The Wild One*, and James Dean, *Rebel Without a Cause*. The style was personal, edgier and a slow shift towards rebellion. Many men took to wearing casual street clothing: knitted pullovers, sleeveless tops, denim jeans, boots and bomber jackets.

There were many Caribbean tailors in Britain that served their local communities, and older men prided themselves on having at least one suit for special occasions such as weddings and funerals. The style of the suit had changed, it was now less formal. The blend of synthetic fibres with natural fibres such as polyester and wool helped to create a lighter, more pliable crease-resistant fabric. The jackets, mostly single-breasted and shorter, had a softer line than the 1940s jackets. The trousers were more tapered and with a pleated waist.

Dressmaking became popular during the late 1950s, another way to keep women in-house. Some Caribbean women were already skilful dressmakers from back home. They were experts in cutting out the fabric shapes free-hand and not requiring patterns. Some bought second-hand sewing machines and became self-sufficient, making clothes for their families and friends in England and in the Caribbean.

Younger Caribbean women went to the local colleges to learn dressmaking. They would purchase paper patterns such as Simplicity, McCall's and Vogue. Fabric lengths, buttons and trims were bought from the Asian travelling salesmen who visited the local homes and from small haberdashery shops and department stores such as Jessops in Nottingham. In the East Midlands there were many fabric-manufacturing companies, so fabrics and trimmings could be purchased cheaply from the local markets.

It was not always easy for the Caribbean and African women to buy off-the-peg garments to fit their shape. The pattern specification for a black female body is slightly different to that of European counterparts. We tend to have smaller, higher waistlines, thicker thighs and higher and more pronounced buttocks. Our unique body shape saw many department stores and fashion shops offering garment-alteration services to their customers.

The primary source of entertainment and family get-togethers were weddings, christenings, anniversaries and birthday parties. These took place in people's homes. We had many such events in my grandfather's house. Women took time out to go to the local hairdresser, which was in someone's home, to have their hair hot pressed and curled. Saturday morning was the preferred day and time, and sometimes going to have your hair done was an all-day social affair.

It was not unusual to hear women complain about the change in the quality of their hair and skin since arriving in Britain. The cold weather and hard water caused the skin to become dry and ashy, and many women complained about dry and thinning hair. The local chemist shops did not cater for us. Homemade coconut hair oil worked well on our scalps and hair in the hot Caribbean climate, but now in the cold, harsh British weather, it solidified on the scalp which could cause hair breakage.

Some hairdressers purchased black hair products, such as Dixie Peach and Posner's Bergamot, from New York for their clients. What stayed with me most since my arrival in 1959 is that powerful image of a Caribbean woman: freshly hot pressed, tightly curled shiny black hair with dark red lipstick teamed with thick, black pencilled eyebrows, finished with the beauty spot. Many women, including my mother, had this look at some point in time. The sultry image of the black music and film stars such as Eartha Kitt, Lena Horne and Dorothy Dandridge inspired many Caribbean women in the 1950s.

▲ Mid-1950s Jamaica – with great-grandmother. © Tuareg Productions

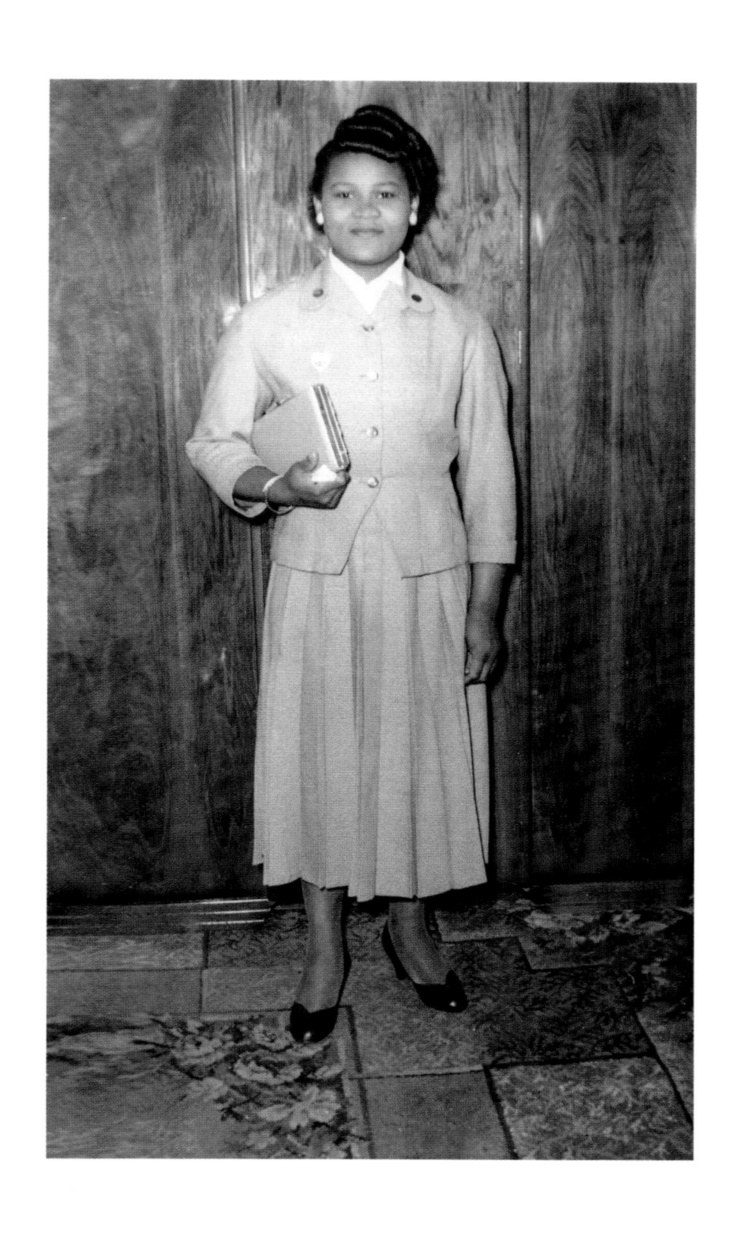

▲ Late 1950s Nottingham – soft tailored suit. © Vida Harris

◀ Late 1950s Jamaica – great-grandmother and young uncles. © Vida Harris

▲ 1956 – Caribbean men in London. © Roger Mayne Archive/Mary Evans Picture Library
◀ 1961 Palisadoes Airport, Jamaica. Courtesy of National Library of Jamaica

▲ 1950s – Caribbean people in London. © Roger Mayne Archive/Mary Evans Picture Library
▶ 1950s – Caribbean women in London. © Roger Mayne Archive/Mary Evans Picture Library

▲ Early 1950s suit. © Maureen Roberts family archives
▶ 1950s Birmingham – full-circle skirt with appliqué short jacket. © Tuareg Productions

▲ Late 1950s North London – dressmaker Mrs Ivy McKenzie. © Carol Williams

▶ Mid-1950s Jamaica – dress made by Mrs Ivy McKenzie in London for her mother-in-law Flandria McKenzie. © Carol Williams

▲ 1950s – bride and groom. © Marsha McDermott family archives
▶ Late 1950s – bride and bridesmaids. © Marsha McDermott family archives

▲ Late 1950s Nottingham – wedding. © Vida Harris
▶ 1950s Birmingham – wedding guests: dresses with full skirts with crinolines; man in double-breasted suit. © Tuareg Productions

▲ Late 1950s Nottingham – bride: powerful image of Caribbean women. © Vida Harris
◄ Late 1950s London – christening: dress with oriental detail. © Beverly Provost OBE

THE 1960s

In 1960, now eight years old, I was a 'roaming flower girl', that's how I felt. Family members and friends planning their weddings would ask my mother for me to be their flower girl, not just in Nottingham, but in Birmingham and London. I guess my early training in standing up straight and looking serious paid off. I was with another girl, similar age and height, and we would each hold a bouquet on either side of the bride.

I remember being packed into the car, mostly sitting on someone's lap, and being driven from one wedding to the next. The wedding dresses in the early 1960s had a full skirt with layers of net, nipped-in waistline, sweetheart neck shape and short or long, fitted sleeves. A long, lace veil was always applied. Towards the late 1960s the form changed drastically, with straighter, fitted, princess-line dresses, with a short shoulder veil. The bridesmaid dresses were always in bright colours – turquoise, lilac and pink were popular. The flower girl's dress, like the one I am wearing in the picture (see page 51), was made from taffeta, trimmed with coloured ribbon.

My step-grandmother, Aunt Lynn, was the local dressmaker. She would make the dresses for the bride, bridesmaids and flower girls. She would skilfully cut freehand the fabric into the garment shapes without a pattern. These were stitched together with her Singer treadle machine. The wedding outfits were fitted to the individual body, to the client's specification.

Since arriving in Nottingham in 1959, I had been the only black pupil at my primary and junior schools. At secondary school, I had two other black girls to connect with, and it was an exciting time for a young 13 year old when youth culture was making its mark.

We had a black-and-white Rediffusion television at home. I remember coming home from school and watching the African-American girl band The Supremes on *Top of the Pops*. Now, these were three girls, stylishly dressed in knee-length, light pink, fitted chiffon dresses. Their hair was jet black and immaculately bouffant. They looked fabulous, and importantly, they were black.

Around the same time in 1964, the original Jamaican rude girl, Millie Small, performed 'My Boy Lollipop' on *Ready Steady Go*. Millie's image was based on the English Mod look: black, tapered ski pants, simple sweater and a casual scarf headband. I had found people on television with the same cultural identity as myself, and I felt proud and for the first time had a sense of belonging.

From an early age, I had wanted to be a dress designer. I loved clothes, loved dressing up and strangely enough the new mod off-the-peg dresses now fitted us. Garment manufacturers started to consider other body shapes when they produced garments; in truth, they finally saw the sale potential from catering to the Caribbean and African communities.

The American beauty company Avon also saw the buying potential of Caribbean women, particularly in the provinces. We had women in our community in Nottingham and Birmingham who became sales agents for Avon, and who earned a living from selling their products to people within their network. They now found beauty products that they could use with confidence. Mothers found it useful as they could work from home in their own time and be free to collect their children from school as, during this time in the UK, families struggled to find childcare.

I have an Aunt Ruby in Birmingham who was a true follower of fashion. She would always bring me the latest mod numbers. I remember my first mod dress, a navy crepe, long-sleeve, flared skirt with white, pleated bib front inset. My next off-the-peg dress was a long-sleeve, check dress with white, flat, Peter Pan collar and cuffs.

Many Caribbean women in the early 1960s took to wearing the typical shift crimplene dress. Crimplene fabric was made up of synthetic fibres, which was another convenient product introduced to help the 'long-suffering' housewife, due to its wash-and-wear properties. During this period, knitting became a favourite pastime for many Caribbean women; thick, cable-style sweaters and cardigans were made for men, women and children. The straight Hobble skirt, worn with knitted twin sets accessorised with a printed scarf was a typical 1960s style.

Tailored dresses for special occasions in brocade fabrics, satins and chiffons were made by local dressmakers. Suits were a favourite for weddings and special occasions. These were the classic short, boxy-style jackets with large buttons and collars, worn with knee-length straight skirts. This outfit was teamed with sizeable patent handbags, white gloves, pillbox hat and kitten heel shoes. The Chanel-inspired, two-piece suit with patch pockets and braided trimming around the edge, worn with a tie-neck blouse and two-tone shoes, was also popular.

The black American influence continued with hair extensions made mostly with yak hair, harvested from the body of the yak. A typical style for the evening was the upsweep bouffant hairstyle, made famous by the African-American soul singer Aretha Franklin and Tamla Motown stars. Yes, now in England we still looked towards America for our beauty and fashion influence.

In the late 1960s, women's fashion changed to another extreme. Miniskirts and shift dresses became much shorter. Hot pants, calf-length platform boots and thick, coloured tights were 'the look'. Jackets and coats in bold check prints, wide collars and lapels were worn. Alongside this was the hippie look, with long dresses, short, fitted bomber jackets and skirts with bright psychedelic prints, tie-dye and floral designs. Tunics and turtleneck tops coordinated with bellbottom trousers were in style. Some Caribbean women started to wear their hair natural as a political statement.

Men's fashion became more relaxed during the early 1960s due to the influence of youth culture. Black youths no longer wanted to dress or socialise with their parents. They now wished to form their own identity. Jamaican music played a significant role in this. Early Ska music by Jamaican artists such as Prince Buster and Desmond Dekker helped to free them from conformity. These two artists, and others who followed with rocksteady and reggae, came with attitude and style. This influenced the way young, black men and other communities dressed in the early 1960s.

The slimline, mohair suit (Ivy League style), made by local tailors, with narrow notch lapel, two or three buttons and centre-back vent was all the rage. The trousers were slim cut, high waisted and worn with ankle pointed-toe boots or shoes. The collarless suit worn by The Beatles in the early 1960s and the 'Tony C' haircut (pointed, peak-style cut) inspired by the American actor Tony Curtis, were favoured by the younger men. Hats, such as the pork pie hat, and later the newsboy and baker boy caps were fashionable. Knitwear was a favourite in the 1960s. Turtle-neck sweaters and cardigans were worn mostly as casual or semi-formal wear.

The late 1960s was a defining time in men's fashion. Fundamental changes were in the jacket lapel, which became more extensive and jackets were mostly double-breasted with double-side back vents. Shirt collars were longer, the Nehru collar – upright mandarin-style – was fashionable on both jackets and shirts. Loose, printed Kaftan-style shirts and tie-dye T-shirts, tunics and wide-flare trousers worn with platform shoes were hipster cool.

Afghan coats and elaborate tunic tops were made famous by the hippy rock style of the African-American musician Jimi Hendrix. The large afro of the African-American actress Marsha Hunt for the West End stage production *Hair* was an important late-1960s black look. In support of the American Civil Rights Movement, James Brown's *Say It Loud – I'm Black and I'm Proud* (1968) was a famous song of the time. Jamaican music reigned supreme in the dance halls and house parties, from bands such as Toots and the Maytals and The Pioneers.

From an early age, I knew the importance of first impressions. I have never felt any sense of racial rejections growing up in Nottingham. However, at times, I could have presented myself more pleasingly. I tried hard to work at this and fashion helped me. It was a way of transforming the person hiding inside. I studied how my young aunts in Nottingham behaved. I looked through fashion magazines, and through TV I was tuned into popular culture.

During my A levels at Arnold College, I decided I needed a weekend job and saved hard – doing odd jobs in the shops in Carlton – to buy a brown, two-piece trouser suit for job interviews. The Odeon Cinema on Angel Row was a modern multi-screen cinema, so having an interest in films, I enquired about weekend work. Dressed to impress in my new trouser suit, I immediately asked for the manager. He seemed impressed with my directness and presentation and offered me the job as an usher. Now my love for films began.

I was in heaven. At that time all the great film classics such as *The Graduate*, *Bonnie and Clyde*, *Butch Cassidy and the Sundance Kid*, *Easy Rider*, *Doctor Zhivago*, *Guess Who's Coming to Dinner* and *Midnight Cowboy* were released in cinemas. I sat and watched for hours, lost in their storytelling, the fashion, the soundtracks and the complete cinematic experience.

My fine art tutor at college told me I was very good at art and design, but I was not encouraged to see it as a profession. I wavered between becoming a fashion illustrator, textile designer or fashion designer. In the end, I was able to incorporate all three options into my future business. The advice from the careers officer was to apply to a garment manufacturing company for an apprenticeship and work my way up. I could do sample machining, pattern cutting, fabric cutting and go to night school to learn fashion designing. I was not keen on this but did try to test the waters by applying to a local dress factory for a trainee post in the fabric-cutting department during the summer holidays.

The supervisor who trained me was extremely patient and dedicated to her company and profession; she suggested that I had a great future in the company. I felt otherwise and could not wait for the bell to ring for tea breaks, lunch and home time each day. The company had two entrances: executives' and workers'. Without thinking about it, I wandered through the executive door; I did not see myself as a factory worker. I was pulled aside by my supervisor and told off for going through the wrong door. Fortunately, the following day, just a few days short of my 18th birthday, I received a letter confirming a place at Derby Art College to do a one-year foundation course.

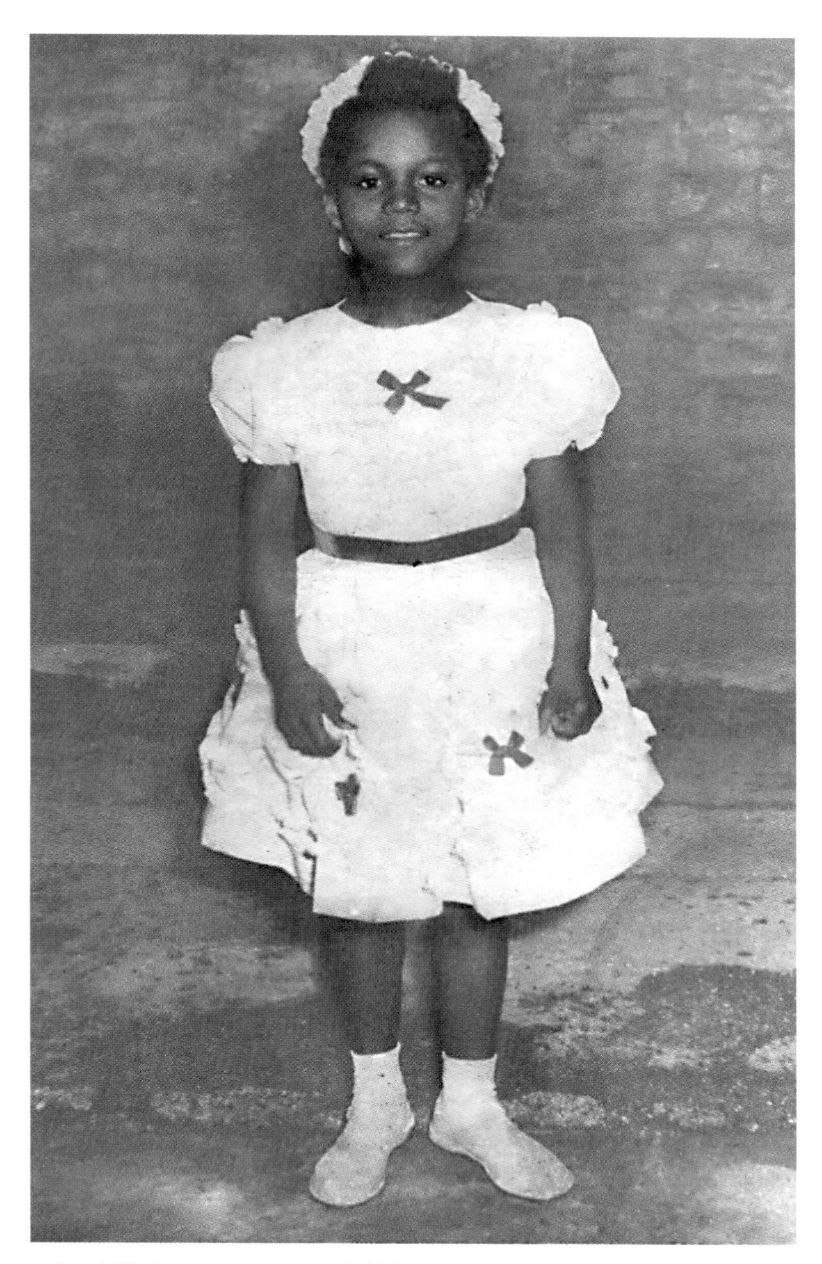

▲ Early 1960s Nottingham – flower girl. © Tuareg Productions

▲ Early 1960s – at junior school in Nottingham. © Vida Harris

▶ Early 1960s mod outfits: white-collar, woollen check suit; short-sleeved, pleated-front dress. Photographer Esmel May Woma © Tuareg Productions/Mary Evans Picture Library

▲ 1960 London – casual wear. © George Fowokan Kelly family archives
◀ Early 1960s – crop pants. © Beverly Provost OBE

▲ Early 1960s Brixton – mohair suit (Ivy League style) made by West End tailor. © George Fowokan Kelly family archives
▶ 1960s – Beatles collarless jacket, tapered trousers, Tony C haircut. © Joseph Williams

▲ 1966 – a Brixton posse. © George Fowokan Kelly
◀ Mid 1960s – mod look, short culottes dress. © Beverly Provost OBE

▲ 1960s Nottingham – thick, knitted cardigan. Photographer: Esmel May Woma
© Tuareg Productions/Mary Evans Picture Library

▶ 1960s – Jacquard knitted sweater. © Yvonne Bell

▲ 1960s – Nottingham wedding: pillar box hats, suits, large handbags. © Phyllis Lewin
▶ 1964 Chelsea, London – wedding. © George Fowokan Kelly

▲ Late 1960s London wedding – slimmer-line dresses for bride and bridesmaids. © Yvonne Bell
◀ Late 1960s – bride with lady in knee-length frock coat and dress. © Yvonne Bell

▲ 1960s Birmingham – Aunt Ruby in mid fur coat and calf-length, pointed-toe boots. © Tuareg Productions
▶ Mid-1960s – one-shoulder maxi dress with cut-out bodice. © Beverly Provost OBE

▲ Late 1960s – taffeta and chiffon dress made by Birmingham dressmaker. © Carmen Reid
◀ Late 1960s – Dashiki (African influence). © Beverly Provost OBE

▲ Late 1960s London – three-quarter-length jacket, straight skirt, kitten heel shoes. © Beverly Provost OBE

◀ Late 1960s – Biba cat suits. © Marsha McDermott

▲ Late 1960s – Biba dress, mohair jacket, striped tie. © Marsha McDermott
◀ Late 1960s London – mohair suit. © Joseph Williams

▲ Late 1960s – bridesmaid; dress made by North London dressmaker Mrs Ivy McKenzie. © Carol Williams
◀ 1960s London. © Olive Graham-Desnoesst family archives

THE 1970s

The Art Foundation course at Derby Art College was not only instrumental in my educational development but also excellent preparation for my future career choices. It was there that I learned about many art forms, other than fashion and textiles: fine art, filmmaking, graphics, music production, photography and media. We studied filmmaking techniques and analysed the works of Orson Welles and the Japanese director, Akira Kurosawa. We investigated the work of the well-known American pop artist Andy Warhol. Our class and lecturers went to London to see his exhibition – my first visit to a London gallery.

The students at Derby Art College came from all over the UK; they were incredibly supportive. I did not feel in any way different, there were no racist comments or feeling of not belonging; we were all there for the love of art. They were mostly from very well-off families, privately educated and some used the course as a finishing school. Very few saw a future in the creative industries. They were at an advantage in that many came from backgrounds where their parents were directors in the creative sectors and thereby able to give them the correct grounding. I came from a working-class background – my stepfather was a coal miner and my mother, a nurse, now a homemaker. My mother laid the foundation for my siblings and me, and as a result I would be the first in my family to receive a university degree.

The grant system for students was different for Foundation Studies then. Our cheques were given to us at the college. I remember two friends and myself collecting our cheques and hitching a ride back into town as college was a few miles away from the city centre. We asked the man in his BMW to drop us off at the Barclays Bank, and I still remember this image of us three students with cheques in hand charging into the bank. The driver thought it was quite amusing, and we clearly showed the spirit and innocence of student life at that time.

I said at the very beginning of the book that the 1970s were eclectic. It was a fusion of cutting-edge culture, with social, industrial and political unrest throughout the country. As art students, we had our own style. Tight-fitted, flared velvet or corduroy trousers and T-shirts were very much in fashion. We were into dyeing individual items of clothing at art college. I remember buying a pair of beige-coloured flares at the beginning of a term and throughout the year dyed them three different colours. I went through the same process with T-shirts by tie-dyeing them and customising them to suit my needs.

Student protest was rife in the 1970s, especially against America's involvement in Vietnam, and in support of the American Civil Rights Movement. Some students took going to protests very seriously, in the way they coordinated their wardrobe. Printed T-shirts with slogans were trendy, such as the iconic, late-1960s images of the Black Panther member and feminist, Angela Davis, and of the revolutionist, Che Guevara. Black youths started to copy the style of the American Black Panthers by wearing black berets, shades and leather jackets. Girls had afros, and wore mostly dark clothes, black leather boots and jackets, with the trademark dark lipstick and gold hooped earrings.

My great aunt in New York had sent me a mohair tunic top as seen in this picture (see page 89), which I wore throughout my art college days. It belonged to my cousin from the mid-1960s. We were very much into mixing new fashion pieces with vintage clothes back then.

We used to go down to London to Laurence Corner, in Camden, to buy ex-army surplus cotton shirts and military-style jackets. The Jimmy Cliff film *The Harder They Come* had a significant effect on me. It confidently told the narrative of that time and place through the choice of street fashion and urban Jamaican music, with its graphic mixing and matching of different clothes, colours, textures and sounds.

It was during the early 1970s when at Derby Art College that we were first introduced to Reggae music. A few months later I saw The Wailers in Birmingham. They played to a tiny audience, and I remember a very stern-looking Bob Marley coming outside to check the short queue. The Rastafari movement, driven by the commercial success of the music of Bob Marley, was the driving force in the popularity of black youth culture in Britain. The wearing of dreadlocks started to become fashionable for men and women in the early 1970s.

The shift to stop straightening our hair and keep it natural, the 'afro', was famous in the 1970s, for both men and women. It was part of our self-discovery, saying, "this is me; I am proud of my heritage". Many women, including myself, had their hair chemically relaxed. I started having my hair relaxed from the late 1970s after graduating. It was a process that allowed me to wash and prepare my hair more quickly, after swimming, going to sleep, and travelling to very humid countries. I did not see it as me trying to be white, or feeling inadequate, but merely a lifestyle choice.

Fashion is a revolving phenomenon, it's hot today and cold tomorrow, never to be taken too literally. A political statement, made in the mid-1960s, allowed the afro to be part of our identity, perfect for that time. Later it became a fashion statement.

Wearing African printed kaftans, studying African history and giving our children African names were also part of that movement. Black music played a significant role in the movement with the song *To Be Young, Gifted and Black* by the African-American singer and Civil Rights activist Nina Simone, being the anthem of the time. We took it further by travelling to various parts of Africa to connect with our roots. It was a period of self and spiritual discovery, and essential for that time.

In 1973, age 20, I had just completed my first year studying Fashion and Textiles at Nottingham Trent Polytechnic, now Nottingham Trent University, and I acquired a student's work permit to go and work in New York over the summer period. I guess it was a form of work placement or internship of the day. The personnel officer took an interest in me going to New York and suggested I contact a former student, Barbara Winters, who had a design company at 229 West 78 Street, New York.

I met up with Barbara in New York and agreed I would start at her company. However, she phoned me a few days before saying her husband had taken ill, and she would be away for a while, meaning that I would be in New York for almost three months without work. I was staying with my great aunt; yes, first mentioned at the beginning who sent parcels to us in Jamaica. She was a senior figure in a girls' reform home in New York and had a house in Brooklyn. The house was divided into three apartments, the first of which was occupied by her daughter and her daughter's children.

Not wanting to stay idle in New York, I decided to look for other summer work. I was watching TV with my great aunt one evening when we saw an advert for Bloomingdale's in Manhattan and I told her I would go there the following day. She exclaimed in her exaggerated American twang, "Bloomingdale's don't employ coloured girls, Lorna".

Defiant, as I am, I went to Bloomingdale's the following day and I was offered the job as a sales consultant, to start immediately. Now to show how little we sometimes know about our communities, the lady who interviewed me for the sales job was a young black woman. My aunt immediately marched her grandchildren out to work commenting, "If Lorna can come here and find work, you all better shape up". Her granddaughter, who was quite happy lying in bed all day, was forced to take heed and got a job, not at Bloomingdale's, but at the less prestigious Alexandra Store. From that moment I realised that I was a leader, not a follower.

Being in New York was a watershed time. Culturally vibrant, yet nothing as I had imagined, and very different from the place I'd passed through in 1959. It was a sweltering summer. The streets of Manhattan were lined with former black American soldiers, unkempt, with missing limbs and begging on the streets. The trains and walls were covered in graffiti. Back in Brooklyn, which was a calm area during the day, I was kept awake on many nights by the sound of gunshots, police sirens and buildings being torched.

These were troubling times, but what transpired from this period of gloom was the unique soul-searching music of the likes of Stevie Wonder, singing about *Living for the City*, with its violence and social injustices. Marvin Gaye was asking questions on *What's Going On?* in America, the reference to the war in Vietnam and saving the environment. Music was played throughout New

York, day and night. The black American artists were documenting the harsh realities of life in America through their music; our choice of clothing became secondary. The perfect-cut T-shirt and jeans were the staple wear, worn with African-inspired costume jewellery. Plaited hair was also in fashion.

Working at Bloomingdale's was a tiring and draining experience and many evenings I missed my stop from falling asleep on the train going back to Brooklyn. It was a cold and distant working environment. The staff dashed from one job to the next; no one talked about the social or political issues, they were oblivious to what was happening around them and the world at large.

Back in the early 1970s, shopping by phone was popular in New York. I worked in the young teens department, and many parents would place the order for their children's clothes for the new school term by phone. These were very affluent Americans, buying six or seven of each item in different colours. They would have been sent a catalogue from the store and were considered loyal customers.

The manager would always call me to deal with the customer on the phone. I would first get a compliment on my accent, "gee your accent is so nice you must be English". I would then have to check in the stockroom to see if what they had ordered was in stock. On one occasion I wandered into the stockroom to find a young black guy filling up a large sack with merchandise, gun in hand. He tells me, "Sister stand back, just helping myself". I stepped aside, frozen, and watched him disappear through the back door.

What I learned from my New York experience was how single-minded the retail business world was. I was forever being told by the manager not to miss a sale. In other words, the moment the customer makes an inquiry, a transaction must follow. This experience helped me to see the fashion industry in a new light. I now saw it as it was, a business. The designer was the first stage in this business alliance to design garments that would sell, and which would keep the company afloat.

I came back from New York recharged and more confident in the fashion course. We were fortunate to have Pauline Denyer, the wife of menswear designer Sir Paul Smith, as our fashion tutor. She was a significant influence on her students; she brought a certain elegance to the course and the fashion industry at large.

In our second year, Pauline arranged for us to go with her to Paris to visit all the dominant fashion houses. She was instrumental in bringing high-profile, industry-based people to lecture in the fashion department. Pauline also brought her former Royal College colleague, the African-American fashion designer Hylan Booker, who taught menswear. It was unusual to find at that time people of colour in the industry. I also remember being taught illustration by the late Colin Barnes, who encouraged me to develop my freehand fashion drawing style. He viewed fashion illustration as an art form. Many years later in my career it helped to open doors and provided me with an income.

In the early to mid-1970s, many Caribbean people who came in the 1940s and 1950s were returning home, including my grandfather, his wife and many family members. The once close Caribbean family unit was breaking up. Watching people left behind to cope without the guidance of their elders was heartbreaking. Young children did not know if they would see their grandparents again, wishing they had taken time out to listen to their stories of coming to Britain. Elders felt guilty for leaving their loved ones behind and apprehensive about the future back home in the Caribbean.

I had met my husband, Errol Holder, in 1973 when he came to visit his brother who was in his final year at Trent. At the end of my second year in the summer of 1974, I decided to get a summer job in a fashion design company. I stayed with Errol who was living at his parents' home in Wembley.

I went for an interview on a Friday morning at a West End design company. The young design director offered me the job in the design room, for the summer. He suggested coming to my house that evening to go through the collection in preparation for Monday. I was kind of naïve and assumed that was how the industry operated. I noticed he was a little surprised when I led him into Errol's mother's Caribbean front room and offered him a cup of tea. We talked for a while about some fabric swatches and sketches he had brought with him. He eventually left and suggested I do some designs ready for Monday. I spent my weekend doing this and looked forward to some experience in the fashion design room.

Monday morning at 8am the phone rang; he told he had changed his mind, no reason given, he just changed his mind. Another time I was offered a job, and again they phoned to say they have changed their minds. The fashion industry was filled with powerful men and women who took advantage of young people starting out in the workplace. Because of this, I have always tried to work hard at my craft, so that I was never judged by or depended on my looks, but by the quality of the work I produced. I was always mindful of not getting too tactile with people I worked with; a handshake is good enough.

In 1975 I graduated from Trent with a BA (Honours) in Fashion and Textile. I was the first black student to graduate with a Fashion and Textile Degree from Trent. I did not go to the graduation ceremony; it did not appeal to me. This was the decade of industrial strikes, three-day week, electricity strike – the future looked bleak. However, I was determined to succeed whatever.

I moved to London, and within a week I was offered my first job at Mono on Curtain Road in the East End, as an assistant to the designer Steven Mono. Mono was a well-established ladies' high-quality suit and coat company, selling mostly to Harrods and Selfridges. The main competitors were Aquascutum and Jaeger. They had a West End showroom on Margaret Street. I had an office to myself and was responsible for drawing the designer's rough sketches into workable drawings, complete with specifications for the master pattern cutters. I was sometimes asked to design a few garments for the collection. On arrival, the production secretary told me she needed to show me how to order buttons. "Buttons!" I exclaimed. Well, I was taken aback, having just graduated with BA (Honours) in Fashion and Textiles, but I ate humble pie and followed her guidance. Many years later I realised how essential buttons are to a garment, and often shared this experience with young designers.

Going to the design room in Margaret Street was interesting as this was where the collection was shown to the primary buyers by the sales directors. Now the sales directors were very powerful; they were responsible for selling the new season's collection to very demanding buyers. They have a portfolio of clients worldwide who purchase garments season by season and to lose a vital buyer is detrimental to a design company.

We had about four House models, who came from a London agency, and many had been modelling for Mono for years. The models parade around the showroom, skilfully drawing the buyers' attention to new design features in the new season's collection. The buyers would make their selection and arrangements would be made to have the garments prepared for dispatch to the required companies.

The Mono brand was not quite couture but high-class fashion. In the late 1970s, it was a dying industry. The women who once bought expensive wool suits and coats with real fur collars and expensive trims were slowly dying out, and the new generation wanted more stylish and practical brands. I moved on from Mono after about six months and started designing and manufacturing my own collection, mostly evening dresses, to be sold in boutiques on the King's Road and in Ohio Rios, Jamaica.

The 1970s youth generation differed significantly from the 1948 Windrush arrivals and those after. We not only wanted to live and work in Britain, but we also wanted our voices to be heard, through political channels to enforce change for a fairer and more equal society. Lovers Rock, known as 'romantic reggae', was the music of black British reggae artists such as Janet Kay, Dennis Brown, Maxi Priest and many others. The dance to this music was slow and intimate. Played in clubs and house parties, Lovers Rock was pure escapism from the turmoil on the streets in inner-city Britain.

The 1976 British drama film, *Pressure*, by black British filmmaker Horace Ové, shows the social and cultural struggles of this generation. It dealt with the many problems first- and second-generation Caribbean youths had to face, such as racism, identity crises and a sense of not belonging. We see the main characters express their anger and grief against the establishment through the choice of clothes and behaviour, showing that the way we dress is the most honest reflection of how we feel inside. This film is an excellent resource for fashion designers, historians and media students to understand late 1970s urban black fashion.

Women's fashion in the mid-to late 1970s was individual, diverse and self-expressive. As a continuation of the late 1960s, we had different skirt lengths: maxi, midi and miniskirts. Popular fabrics were synthetics, cottons, corduroy, lace, embroidery and patchwork denim. These were printed in swirling psychedelic designs, tie-dye effects, floral designs and bold geometric prints.

Maxi halter-top dresses, lurex camisole tops, striped ribbed sweaters, fringed suede tunics, hot pants, hipster jeans, wide-brim hats and platform shoes were worn during the early to mid-1970s. Mid- to late-1970s fashion was soft, long and flowing, particularly for weddings and special occasions. The maxi skirt in printed fabrics was still worn, teamed with fitted, long-sleeve blouses, high collars and wide cuffs. During the later 1970s, the style switched to a more moderate look, to accommodate the new working women. Fitted, tailored camel jackets, wide-leg trousers, shirt dresses, A-line skirts, silk blouses and high-waisted, leather trousers were worn.

The look for men was comfortable casual wear; high-waist, semi-flared jeans, colourful, knitted, short sleeveless pullovers, dashiki (West African shirts), casual, Indian collarless tops, fitted denim shirts, accessorised with Rastafari-inspired, coloured knitted hats and scarves. Loose, suede, patchwork jackets and tailored leather jackets were also fashionable, worn alongside platform shoes and leather peaked caps.

The late 1970s saw the influence of John Travolta in *Saturday Night Fever*. Light-coloured, three-piece suits, with wide collars and lapels, flared trousers, colourful shirts with wide-pointed collars, soft, wide ties and platform shoes were the fashion. More men were wearing sportswear as an everyday fashion.

We now see how fashion and music helped the young black British youths form their own identity; a fusion of the Caribbean, African, American and British.

Errol and I bought a three-bedroom, semi-detached house in Hayes, and on 10 July 1976 we got married. I shifted from the old family traditions. We did not get married in a church, as expected, but at Harrow Register Office. Instead of having a dress made, I bought a Janice Wainwright cream embroidered kaftan from a boutique on the King's Road. My Russian wedding ring was bought from a jeweller on the same street. Headscarves/wraps were still very fashionable, so I made a long, cream, silk scarf to match the dress. Errol wore a cream silk, three-piece suit teamed with brown striped high-collar shirt and wide tie (see pages 102 and 103).

I mentioned earlier that I had sold evening dresses to a boutique in Ohio Rio, Jamaica. Well, we had our honeymoon in Ohio and stayed at the Hilton. On leaving the hotel, we entered a charming shop only to find my dresses on display, bought by a Jamaican businesswoman who worked for Air Jamaica.

I am a great believer in taking up opportunities, so when Errol was offered a job for the Omani Television in November 1976, off we went. I decided to partner with the Omani Finance Officer and managed the Ali Baba boutique in Salalah. I travelled to many places to buy products: Cyprus, New York, Dubai and back to London. Oman had a sizeable Asian workforce, so I bought the local fabrics and the Asian tailors made the garments for the shop. The clients were mostly French, German, American and English expatriates.

The Holiday Inn in Salalah gave me a showcase where I exhibited local Omani antique silver jewellery. It was a great way to preserve their heritage. The highlight of my stay in Oman was that I staged the first televised fashion show at the Holiday Inn. The outfits were all made locally, from fabric sourced locally, and modelled by expatriates.

On returning to the UK in November 1978, I was very much in demand as a head designer due to my business and leadership skills acquired over the years.

I worked for a Birmingham-based company, House of Lerose, and ran their new design studio on Lexington Street in Soho, London. They specialised in classical ladies' soft suits and dresses.

The British fashion industry was going through significant changes and women now wanted practical casual wear. New developments in fabrics and manufacturing techniques abroad made it hard for British manufacturers to compete. The high cost of garment production in Britain, disruptive strikes and poor sales meant most British-based companies had to move their production abroad or close. Lerose decided to close the design studio in London.

▲ Early 1970s Nottingham – student; mohair tunic top from America; afro hair. © Tuareg Productions

▲ Early 1970s London – T-shirt and corduroy fitted jeans. © Billie Ohene
▶ 1970s London – hot pants, short, floral, fitted bomber jacket, high two-tone boots. © Beverly Provost OBE

▲ 1970s London – afro hair, turtle-neck sweater, knee-length straight skirt, wide-collar fitted jacket, check Oxford bags. © Olive Graham-Desnoes

◀ 1970s Nottingham – Levi jeans with braces. © Vida Harris

▲ 1970s North London – students. © Billie Ohene

◀ Early-1970s Nottingham – art student: soft, sheer, printed fabrics, bias-cut skirt, platform shoes. © Tuareg Productions

▲ Early 1970s Brixton – platform shoes, patchwork leather jacket. © George Fowokan Kelly
▶ Early 1970s Nottingham – Aunt Lynn, community dressmaker. © Vida Harris

▲ Early 1970s London – great aunt and uncle at their son's wedding. © Joseph Williams
▶ 1970s London – Caribbean bride and American marine groom. © Yvonne Bell

▲ 1970s London – abstract print maxi skirt. © Yvette Holder

◀ Mid-1970s London – bride in blue; long, flowing fashion and tailored 1940s retro look. © Tuareg Productions

▲ Mid-1970s – my wedding day with Mum; long, flowing styles. © Tuareg Productions
▶ Mid-1970s, Harrow, London – wedding day. © Tuareg Productions

▲ Late 1970s London – wedding reception at home. © Tuareg Productions

◄ Late 1970s – great aunt and uncle; printed maxi dress, three-piece, pin-stripe suit. © Vida Harris

▲ Late 1970s Nottingham – jacket with wide collar and lapels; sweater and tie; afro hair. © Chris Harris
◀ 1970s London – maxi skirts, halter and lurex tops. © Yvonne Bell

▲ Late 1970s London – wedding guests, with ladies in soft, flowing styles. © Tuareg Productions
▶ Late 1970s London – velour track suit, corduroy trousers. © Tuareg Productions

▲ Late 1970s – other cultural influences: Arab cotton desert scarf. © Tuareg Productions

◀ Late 1970s – camel tailored jacket, full skirt, leather bomber jacket, turtle-neck sweater and flared trousers. © Tuareg Productions/Mary Evans Picture Library

▲ Late 1970s Oman – Indian silk collarless shirt. © Tuareg Productions/Mary Evans Picture Library
▶ Late 1970s – fitted, high-waist leather pants, bold print scarf. © Root Magazine

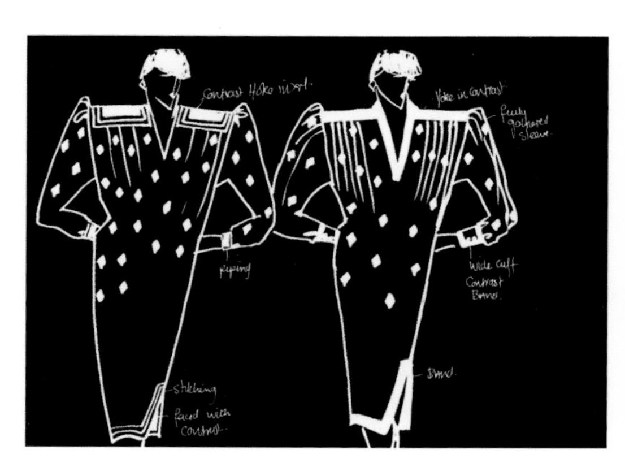

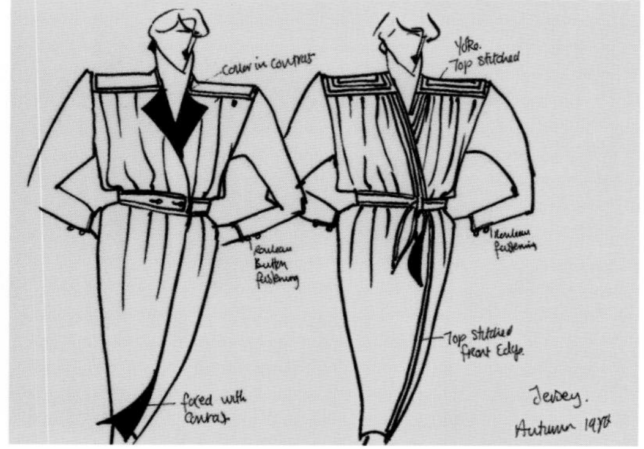

▲ 1980s fashion sketches by Lorna Holder © Tuareg Productions

Collar in Contrast
Shaped cuff
Side panel in Contrast
Contrast Shaped cuff
Faced with Contrast

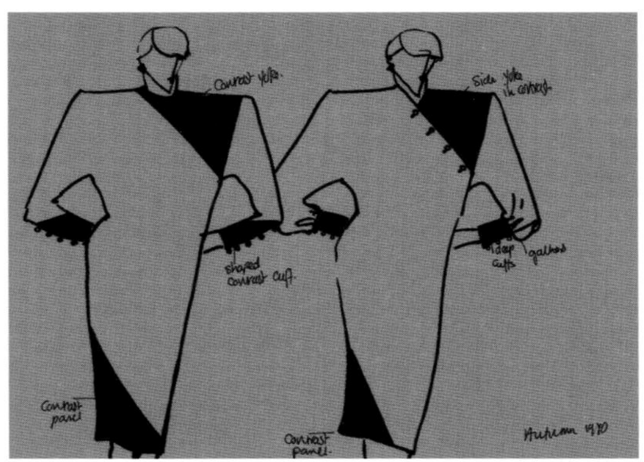
Contrast yoke.
Side yoke in contrast
shaped contrast cuff.
Contrast panel
Contrast panel.

THE 1980s

In 1980, at the age of 27, I became the Head of Young Fashion for one of the Raybeck companies, Davies and Field, based in London on Bethnal Green Road; the same building now occupied by Rich Mix. I joined Davies and Field after my agent arranged an interview with the Managing Director, Mr Harold Davies. The meeting went well, and I waited to hear back from him. A day or so later I received a telegram, asking for me to come to see them. I was offered the job as Head of Young Fashion, to start immediately.

It transpired that the former designer who had been there a while, and was one of the directors, had left to form another company; now an immediate competitor. The pressure was on for me to manage the fashion department, and to design the various collections without any top management guidance. It was a process of learning on the job.

I cannot say I did not have problems at the beginning because I had joined a design team who had worked for the former designer and they were resentful – I was now in her place. The activist would say the problem was racial, I thought differently. I was a 27-year-old black woman who looked 20 years old and was put in charge of white women, many of whom were in their late 50s or early 60s. It was a post-war generation that equated experience with age. I had to be sensitive to each person's need and resolute in getting the work done. I had to work harder and always prove myself, not only to the design room staff but to the production staff, buyers and some fabric manufacturing representatives.

Mindful of the constant scrutiny, I made sure I mastered my profession to the best of my abilities. Going to work on time was vital. I was in the design studio earlier than most people. I made sure my scheduled appointments with fabric reps were on time to save them queuing up outside my office. Above all, I made sure I delivered that winning number that sold, in thousands. I achieved this by keeping abreast of the current trends, understanding the needs of the client, and never being fearful of experimenting with new technical developments in textiles and with the manufacturing of garments. I took work home most nights and produced most of the designs from home. I always experimented with new fabrics. I would first cut out a rough shape, see how it hangs, drapes, pleats and how it reacts after washing; all this in my own time.

Davies and Field were one of the UK's largest dress manufacturers. I was responsible for the young Justin range and some older women's designs, supplying Littlewoods mail order, Littlewoods chain stores, Kays Catalogue, Etam, Lady at Lord John's, Berkertex and the large department store on Oxford Street – Bourne & Hollingsworth. We had another designer who worked on the opposite side of the large design room. She worked part-time for the older women's fashion.

Davies and Field mass-produced dresses and soft suits. I managed the department with a team of sample pattern cutters, sample machinists, sample cutter and a design assistant. I was responsible for designing the various collections – selecting and purchasing all the fabrics and trims – and having the design made for the first showroom samples, to show to the buyers.

It was a new experience working in the garment mass-production market, where fabric, trimmings and production time kept within a given budget. I had to create designs that could be repeated season by season, with a simple change of collar shape, raised or dropped hemline, change of sleeve length or sleeve taken out, or just adding a belt and more. These garments were produced in the thousands and bought by women and young girls who wanted to look fashionable at a low cost. The Littlewoods catalogue was the equivalent to online shopping today, with a difference. It offered the customer the choice of paying in small instalments for their purchases.

Many Caribbean families had these catalogues at home and were their preferred choice of shopping. Modern fabric developments, together with cutting-edge designs and clever progressive pattern cutting, allowed the fabrics to stretch and fit a variety of body shapes. There were more colour choices for a range of skin tones, and we became more experimental in our selection of fashion coordination. It was a move forwards.

The women I was designing for were very much the women I went to secondary school with, in the late 1960s. It was a culture of leaving school or college with shorthand and typing or nursing skills, getting married and having children. In our family, we all had bought our own houses, because that was very much part of our heritage. Spending four years at an art college studying fashion was seen by many as utter madness. My mother, however, encouraged me to be different and follow my dreams.

As a designer, I spent much of my time travelling – to Paris every 12 weeks to the various shows, and to New York, Hong Kong and Germany. It was essential to visit the shops in the West End to see what other brands were up to, to keep up with the general news, people and lifestyle. I also made many visits to galleries and kept abreast of what was showing at the cinemas.

We were now in the early 1980s, and the most significant influence on commercial women's fashion was Princess Diana. Our clients adored the simple, frilly collars and cuffs and the soft, flowing hemlines she wore, and we were forced to keep producing such styles.

However, at the same time in Britain we had a period of black social and political unrest and clashes with the establishment, which were reflected in our everyday look. Black British youths influenced by the American hip-hop music and style, which originated in South Bronx, USA, took heed. Others continued with the Black Panther look, with berets and leather jackets from the 1970s.

It was the fashion explosion of tight, high-waisted faded jeans, partnered with oversize, shapeless tops, and finished with what defined the 1980s, designer sneakers. Oversized accessories, heavy gold chains, multiple rings and Kangol hats, made famous by rapper LL Cool J, were the rage. To complement this movement, both men and women wore the Jheri curl, a loose hair perm with a shiny wet appearance, developed for black hair. Hip-hop broke all the fashion rules and put black American youth culture firmly on the global map.

Showing diversity in the fashion styles of the early 1980s, alongside the hip-hop craze, we had the American 1950s retro 'preppy' look. This was the wearing of brightly coloured clothes: polo shirts, Oxford shirts with button-down collars, turtlenecks, sleeveless v-neck sweaters, chinos, high-waisted, peg-legged jeans, boxy jackets, classical raincoats and white sneakers.

Fashion for women was just as varied and dynamic. We saw the emphasis on broad, padded shoulders. Fabrics were glitzy synthetics in bold colours and abstract shapes. The hair was either high volume, big and bouncy or short and spiky, a follow on from the 1970s punk look. The geometric flat top fashioned by Jamaican singer and model Grace Jones was well copied. Baggy and oversized T-shirts now teamed with leggings or high-waisted, tapered jeans. The short, flounced rah-rah skirts and dresses, worn with leg warmers, thick fishnet tights, short, colourful bomber jackets and miniskirts, were an instant hit in young fashion. During this period, we saw the demand for velour leisurewear tracksuit tops and bottoms, bright fabric headbands, florescent lipsticks and two-tone shoes.

The 1940s retro look was sharp also in the 1980s, focusing on straight skirts, hip-length jackets with shoulder pads, small collars and lapels. Many Caribbean girls took to pinning up their hair in the style of the 1940s and wearing large, bright clip-on earrings. Grunge fashion – timeless, loose and androgynous – was favourite among the young. The most common feature was the wearing of T-shirts under large, open shirts with jeans. The trend for both men and women had no season, no definition, no night or day, no right or wrong!

This period of fashion was not a smooth look for me to interpret into producing mass-produced garments. It was also not a big commercial seller. Our primary clients still wanted the pretty, safe dresses and soft suits that they had become accustomed to. I did, however, introduce some street cred alongside our leading collection, with a small feature such as broad, padded shoulders, shift dresses and strong geometric fabric prints.

It was during this period that many commercial fabric printers produced Italian-inspired bold tapestry and border prints on synthetic fabrics. The availability of these prints made a massive contribution to the 1980s commercial fashion. The focus was on keeping the shape very simple and letting the bold prints with broad, padded shoulders do the work.

Further development of stretch fabrics: spandex and velour, enabled the leisurewear market to flourish. We had mass-produced garments such as straight, tight, tube skirts, tight, shiny, fitted pants and the ever-popular boob tube. The use of soft, fleecy fabrics for sporty dresses and skirts was prevalent, giving the wearer the option of teaming it with leg warmers or tying a sweater around the shoulders. We produced garments towards the end of the 1980s that allowed the wearer to invent their look, which celebrated diversity in fashion, unlike the 1940s, 1950s and 1960s when the style was regimented.

While at Davies and Field I had our first son, Warren, in 1983, seven years after getting married. I had worked with the company for more than four years, which was unusual for an industry known for showing you the door after one season. The fashion industry in the 1980s did not cater for the needs of the professional working woman. I worked right up to giving birth; I left work in the evening and had my son the following morning. Since graduating in 1975, I had worked nonstop, yet the fear of being unemployed was daunting.

It was during the time of Margaret Thatcher (UK Prime Minister 1979-90), a symbol of female power, yet for some women that power had value only in the workplace. The 1980s was not a time that gave credit to the stay-at-home mother. We were financially sound, owned our own four-bedroom apartment in West Hampstead and drove two cars, but I was afraid to give up work. So, I did what my managing director proposed, "have six weeks off work for maternity leave, get a nanny and get right back to work Lorna".

My son, Warren, at a very early age, was familiar with seeing me drawing. He took to drawing also, and at the age of four at school was runner-up for a Cadbury's competition. He became a very successful graphic designer/ illustrator in the film industry.

In the early 1980s few manufacturers did in-house manufacturing. Most of the garments were farmed out to outdoor workers to make. Many of these outdoor workers had machines at home, labouring hard, stitching up the various sections of the garments for very little pay. This method of manufacturing was called 'piece work'. The fashion world outside was evolving, but the people who were responsible for the early manufacturing stages were archaic and inward thinking. I was glad I chose the higher education route after school, otherwise trying to work my way up to become a designer in the industry would never have happened.

I was at the top of my profession; but it was a lonely existence. We talk today about diversity in the workplace, but I had never met any other black designers in senior positions in London during my time in the industry. We had a few pattern cutters, graders, sample machinists, fabric stock cutters, perhaps showroom salespeople working for other large design companies. There were a few independent men's and ladies' wear designers.

Towards the late 1980s, five out of my eight siblings followed my journey and worked in the fashion and creative industries. Chip: men's wear designer/ lecturer; John: fashion stylist/furniture designer; Elaine: fashion advertising; Christopher: photographer; and Hannah: modelling.

Women's fashion in the late 1980s was still very extreme but now had a purpose. In the past decades, particularly the 1950s and 1960s, women's fashion centred on the home, or how we dressed to go to church, collect the children from school, go to the cinema or the local dance. In the late 1980s, more women were now going out to work. Women were more confident in the workplace and the style revolved around the job. We continued to use our clothes to express ourselves. Caribbean women were finding work in advertising, television and media, politics, local authorities, education, fashion merchandising and retailing. More women were buying their own homes independently, having holidays abroad and taking control of their futures.

The intention was to be a part of the male-dominated world. The style for women was masculine and empowering; the language was New York aggression. We became fitness fanatics; hair was full and high, cut very short or gelled back. We were spending more money on beauty treatments, eating out and in wine bars than ever before. We smoked and drank more, and some women never talked about babies unless a nanny was in context. It seemed to be a superficial, money-obsessed culture.

Buying expensive, designer-labelled handbags, sunglasses, shoes, jewellery, clothes and sportswear constituted 'power dressing'. Celebrity-endorsed fashion as seen on billboards, in magazines, on television drama series such as *Dallas*, and MTV music videos determined what we wore. The late 1980s was a period when the fashion model Naomi Campbell, of Jamaican heritage, was the first black model on the cover of French *Vogue*. She has contributed significantly to the enhancement of women of colour in fashion.

Long, wide-shouldered jackets and oversized coats were even more prominent. Blanket shawls became popular, creating a much-layered look. Black leather trousers or pencil skirts, teamed with brightly coloured jumpers with padded shoulders were very much part of the winter wardrobe for women.

Dresses also had very wide shoulders, small collars, and the waistline held in with wide belts, or cummerbunds. Mid-calf-length straight skirts as well as short, leather mini skirts and leggings were the look of choice. For added embellishment, large, drop earrings were an essential feature together with applied make-up.

To contrast this movement, a famous brand for professional women, especially during the summer season both for work and leisure, was Williwear by African-American designer Willi Smith. Williwear was my favourite designer brand:

comfortable fit, well-made blouses, jackets, culottes and oversize tops in Indian cotton; Madras checks, signature colours in browns, beige, khaki and rust.

Fashion created a culture which saw a power switch between genders. In the late 1980s, men's fashion had a softer line. The jacket, still somewhat loose, had a narrower shoulder line. The soft, original military-style jacket with large patch pockets and shoulder strap detail in khaki was worn. The technique was to roll or push the sleeves up and to wear plain, silky T-shirts in pastel colours under jackets with Ray-Ban sunglasses. Trousers had a pleated front and a loose-fitted and high waist. Black leather, studded jackets had now been made fashionable by Michael Jackson. Colourful tracksuits were also in style. Nike ruled in the urban footwear. The signature hairstyle for young, black guys of the late 1980s was the high-top fade – this was king.

In 1986 I decided to leave Davies and Field. Career-wise I had come to a full stop and could not grow any further in the company. I was expecting my second son, Julian, and wanted a profession where I could have the freedom to look after my children and work without the feeling of guilt from being a working mother.

I had an interest in the beauty and hair business combined with retailing of accessories and gifts. We opened the Lapaz shop on Camden High Road. A year later we opened the Notting Hill Gate branch.

▲ 1980s London – with young design team at Davies and Field. © Tuareg Productions
▶ Early 1980s London – Princess Diana influence, Littlewoods mail order selection. © Tuareg Productions

F
£24·99
G
£29·99
dress by Justine with elasticated
and self belt. Length 43 ins. See
Fabric: woven blend with glitter
Washable. Fibre: 55% acrylic,
Red. GD 307 Dress
12, 14, 16 £23·99 20 wks £1·20
tty dress by Justine with broderie
glaise trimming at neck and cuffs
43 ins. See size chart. Fabric: woven
that's warm to the touch. Washable
20% wool, 80% mixed fibres. Blue.
2 Dress
10, 12, 14, 16 £24·99 20 wks £1·25
Two-piece suit by Justine has pleated
skirt. Broderie anglaise trimming at
and cuffs. Skirt length 27 ins
luding waistband). See size chart.
ric: woven blend that's warm to the
ch. Dry clean. Fibre: 20% wool, 80%
ed fibres. Red tartan. GD 317 Skirt suit
es 10, 12, 14, 16 £29·99 20 wks £1·50
CHECK MATE
THE NEW LOOK FROM Justine

RTAULDS FIBRES
Tricel.
Viloft
COURT

▲ 1980s London – fashion show; designed for Courtelle. © Tuareg Productions
◀ 1980s fashion show – soft, frilly skirt and bustier, designed for Courtelle. © Tuareg Productions

▲ 1980s – pretty frilly look. Photographer Newton Maxwell Harris © Root Magazine
▶ 1980s – colour block: short skirt, wide shoulders, head tie. © Root Magazine

▲ 1980s London – Michael Jackson-inspired leather jacket; girls having fun. © Brian Clarke
▶ Early 1980s Nottingham – denim rah-rah dress. © Chris Harris

▲ Early 1980s – hip-hop influence: short leather skirt, head bands. © Root Magazine
◀ 1980s – black leather, strapless dress, leather jacket and pleated front trousers. Photographer Lloyd R Jones © Root Magazine

▲ Early 1980s London – dressed for demonstration. © Billie Ohene
◀ Early 1980s London – early power dressing. © Gene Huie-Manneh

▲ Early 1980s London – young people hanging out. © Michael A Wells
▶ Mid-1980s London – two looks: double-breasted, pin-stripe, wide collar and lapel tailored suit; vintage military jacket. © Brian Clarke

▲ 1980s – crop, stone-wash jeans. © Billie Ohene
▶ Early 1980s Nottingham – 1940s influence. © Chris Harris

▲ Early 1980s Germany – baggy sweat top, crop jeans, two-tone shoes. © Elaine Harris
◀ 1980s Nottingham – straight skirts, wide belts. © Chris Harris

▲ Mid 1980s London – young people hanging out. © Olive Graham-Desnoes
▶ 1985 – grunge look. © Root Magazine

▲ Early 1980s Nottingham – T-shirt and shirt combination. © Elaine Harris
▶ 1980s – 1940s-inspired up-sweep hairstyle, wide shoulders and accessories. © Root Magazine

▲ Mid-1980s – bride and groom. © Mr and Mrs Williams
◀ Mid-1980s London – 1930s-inspired wedding dress. © Billie Ohene

▲ 1980s London – bride; wedding dress with wide shoulders. © Elaine Maull Robinson
▶ 1980s Nottingham – mannish double-breasted jacket and tie-neck blouse. © Carol Williams

▲ Late 1980s London – Lapaz hair fashion shoot. © Tuareg Productions
▶ Late 1980s London – Lapaz fashion shoot, spiky hair, wide shoulders. © Tuareg Productions

▲ 1980s London – satin Jacquard dress with gold accessories. © Carol William
◀ Late 1980s Nottingham – bold colours, spiky hair, big earrings. © Elaine Harris

▲ Late 1980s – Lapaz hair weave promotion. © Tuareg Productions
◀ Late 1980s London – Lapaz image natural hair weave. Photographer Damian Walker © Tuareg Productions

THE 1990s

In the early 1990s, Caribbean men and women were spending more money on hair, beauty and fashion accessories and were quick to try new trends and products. The Lapaz shops were a one-stop outlet for hair extensions, beauty treatments, sunbeds and beauty and fashion retailing.

The hair extensions we did were the natural hair weave, which was preferred by the professional business women. Unlike today, when it's obvious that a woman is wearing a wig or a weave hair extension, in the early 1990s it was our little secret. Many women claimed that they did not tell their workmates, partners or husbands they had extensions. How they kept this a secret is still a mystery to me.

We had one situation when a young woman of mixed heritage came into the Camden salon to have her long curly weave taken out, and new hair weaved in. She left instructions with the receptionist not to let her English boyfriend come down to the lower ground where she was having her hair done. The receptionist went to collect something from the back of the salon. The boyfriend arrived at the shop and went downstairs to find his girlfriend without her usual flowing locks. He apparently did not know she wore extensions. The lack of understanding of other cultural habits and needs, magnified in this situation, is a perfect example of how personal and entrenched our sense of identity is in Britain.

Another type of hair extension we specialised in was the Monofibre, which is an acrylic fibre, famous for dreadlocks or worn long and straight; multicoloured for the Camden club culture and grunge look.

From the late 1970s, natural hair dreadlocks were the style of choice for many black musicians. London-based groups such as Soul to Soul and Steel Pulse, the

Birmingham roots reggae bands, and the singer Eddy Grant were examples of black musicians who wore the natural dreads. Some band members, such as Bob Marley, wore dreads because of their spiritual identity. However, in the 1990s it became more of a fashion statement for both black and white people.

In the early 1990s, both men and women travelled more for business and leisure. We saw further developments in synthetic fabrics: trousers, skirts, jackets, coats and tailored suits, made from lighter-weight fabrics with drip-dry, non-iron and crease-resistant properties. Ladies' shoes, boots and handbags, made from high-grade engineered fabrics, created an informal minimalistic look.

The 1950s and 1960s retro look became more pronounced during the early 1990s, for both men and women, when fashion designers and people in the creative industries adapted it for everyday wear. This was the wearing of dark denim, straight-cut jeans, cropped pants, black polo neck sweaters, black leather jackets, striped Nordic T-shirts and the trademark black berets. Many people confused this style with the Black Panther fashion, but it was based on the American beatnik style.

I had designed and produced a collection of Lycra wear and bought for the shops a range of accessories and bags, which were very popular with our clients. The look was the basic high-waist black leggings, coordinated with a halter-neck top and a well-tailored, black jacket. I added silver eyelets on the outside leg and a range of prints. The collection included a very short Lycra tube mini skirt worn with thick, black opaque tights and a mini sleeveless dress with silver eyelets, worn with black fishnet tights.

We sold the thick, over-knee stockings, worn with short, pleated check skirts, a favourite item in the young woman's wardrobe. Costume jewellery, usually thick rows of pearls and drop earrings, was highly sought after. Bum bags, backpacks, headbands and fabric scrunchies for putting up the hair were also fashionable. Long, leather gloves were in demand worn with biker leather jackets. Early to mid-1990s saw a more business-like approach to fashion for both men and women.

For women, the bright, abstract colours of the late 1980s were now mostly black, navy and pastel. The long, tailored jacket with padded shoulders, worn with leggings or short skirts, remained popular. The jacket shape was still 'mannish' but based on the classic 1940s cut.

The high-street fashion shops were now stocking merchandise from Asia, particularly from India and China. Many British fashion houses started having their garments made in India at competitive prices. Indian cotton and silks were in high demand, in spicy Indian shades. Long, silky scarves were versatile accessories, worn wrapped around the head, the waist or tied to a bag.

My favourite mid-1990s, Indian-inspired garments were the jodhpurs, named after the State of Jodhpur. These were made of linen, in natural shades of khaki, cream, brown and tan. They are a great shape for accentuating the waistline, especially worn with a leather belt or silk scarf and soft, flat, leather, lace-up shoes and sandals.

Another favourite was the Nehru jacket, named after Prime Minister Jawaharlal Nehru (first Prime Minister of India after independence). This shape was also a stylish jacket and shirt style for men in the late 1960s. The version for women was more fitted with a small stand collar, patch pockets and buttons down the front, mostly made in linens or silks. It was a versatile style in that you could wear it open with a T-shirt or vest underneath or button through. Other versions based on the Nehru jacket were looser and longer (tunic style), which still had the stand collar, no pockets and worn with leggings or jeans.

Branding and marketing and the association with famous logos came to prevalence in the late 1990s. We saw a change in the type of garments created for the high street. The popularity of hip-hop saw rappers such as Snoop Dogg, Puff Daddy and Coolio working with major fashion brands: Timberland, Reebok, Kangol, Champion, Hilfiger and Fila. Many artists later created their fashion labels – Kanye West (Yeezy) and Diddy (Sean John and Enyce). The overall theme was "the bigger, the better". Jeans were cut multiple sizes too big, with large, patch back pockets, to show off branding.

Other fashion items favoured by Caribbean youths were Timberland boots, polo shirts, Hilfiger sweatshirts, leather bomber jackets and baggy dungarees; cropped denim jackets for women with silver-coloured jewellery and the quintessential Nike brand trainers. American hip hop continued to have a massive influence on British Caribbean youth culture.

We had the Lapaz shops for nine years and closed in 1995. It was another turning point in my life. I had my youngest son, Miles, in 1991; the two eldest were at secondary school, and I now wanted to work from my studio at home. I started designing an exclusive line for clients who responded to my advert placed in English *Vogue* and *Brides* magazine. The garments I designed and created were business dresses and suits, evening and bridal wear made from designer fabrics. The clientele were mostly affluent people of all nationalities.

I had a pattern cutter, off the premises, who made the patterns from my sketch and specification, and a machinist who made them up in my studio. The studio was on two floors in my house, and a great way to work and look after my family. It was vital for me to be at home with teenage boys, of black heritage, growing up in London. They never had any reason to stray after school. Warren, Julian and Miles were incredibly cooperative and respectful when I had clients. They would do their homework or play on their computers in their room without a sound. I think this was the best professional/family decision I have ever made, and it paid well in later years. Once again, I made it happen.

▲ 1990s – Lycra wear worn with Moroccan top, curly hair extension. © Tuareg Productions
▶ Early 1990s London – monofibre dreadlocks. Photographer Damian Walker © Tuareg Productions

▲ 1990s – mannish jacket and jodhpurs. © Tuareg Productions

◀ 1990s New York – layered look: high-waist, stirrup trousers, flat shoes. Photographer Errol Holder © Tuareg Productions

▲ 1990s – Chip: Beatnik influence. © Chip Harris
▶ 1990s – black and grey tones; leggings, T-shirt, bum bag, baseball cap, straight cut jeans. © Chip Harris

BLACK

Picasso

▲ 1990s London – two generations: bold fashion statements. © Veronica McKenzie
◀ 1990s London – Beatnik look. © Tuareg Productions

▲ 1990s London – Lycra wear designed for the Lapaz shops. © Tuareg Productions
▶ 1990s London – straight hair weave, monochrome fashion. © Tuareg Productions

▲ Mid-1990s Nottingham – themed wedding look. © Mrs Andrea Weaver
◀ 1990s London – wedding guests, themed look: off-the-shoulder, layered, net-enhanced, drop-waist dress. © Yvonne Bell

▲ 1990s London – Lapaz fashion shoot: other ethnic influences. ©Tuareg Productions

▶ Mid-1990s London – natural weave extension, bold crystal clustered earrings with matching bracelet; Lapaz shop. Photographer Damian Walker © Tuareg Productions

2000 TO THE PRESENT DAY

In the early 2000s, the Caribbean men and women were into dressing up for that unique occasion, so different from previous decades when 'dressing up' was limited to the house parties, weddings and christenings held in our homes or church halls. We would now go with confidence to special gala dinners, award ceremonies, graduation ceremonies, community events, music events and festivals.

We were taking more annual holidays, visiting our families in the Caribbean and meeting up with friends to go on cruises. Young people were now travelling globally, exploring faraway places. We had more influences than just our immediate families, TV and film. We now had access to the Internet, allowing us to be more experimental in the fusion of fashion from diverse global cultures. The internet was the powerhouse driving us towards celebrity culture – watching what famous people wear and trying to emulate their lifestyle.

The early 2000s is also the period when student graduation ceremonies became an 'industry', with young women and men splashing out to buy their very first graduation outfits. For many girls, purchasing that unique pair of super high-heel shoes was a new experience, likewise for many boys a tailored suit, jacket or designer tie.

During this decade we see another type of high-street brand collaboration. Major high-street chains such as Top Shop, H&M and Marks & Spencer partnered with actors, models and home-grown celebrities to help promote their brands. This association helped to provide affordable, designer-inspired, off-the-peg garments for both men and women.

The emphasis on how to show off the well-toned female body was the key in the early 2000s. The neckline, both for day and evening wear, was now plunged low and revealing. The market for push-up bras and breast implants multiplied, bringing the female breast into centre frame. Evening wear for special occasions featured prolonged and mid-length sexy, sparkly, revealing dresses to show off toned curves. The skirts and dresses were short and clinging, without the 1960s innocence, worn with the signature backbreaker, high-heeled shoes. We saw the elevation of the designer brand, low-rise boot-cut and skinny jeans, not just for everyday wear but teaming with designer crop, beaded halter tops, fitted denim tops, designer T-shirts and little leather or suede jackets for special occasions.

This decade saw more African-inspired ladies' fashion. Many high-street brands such as Zara, H&M and New Look incorporated an African theme within their collection. We had African fashion houses producing dresses online and for shops in African prints, based on the contemporary high-street shapes. Brands used African prints on T-shirts, allowing the wearer to coordinate with jeans, favourite trainers and backpack; an ideal look in street fashion. Mature Caribbean women still adorned their outfits with African shawls and accessories, a flashback to the late 1970s. African prints, now taken seriously, have a bright future in high-street fashion because they are timeless and adaptable.

Men were also into showing off the sculptured body. Tattoos have had a significant impact on popular culture, announcing the freedom to do what one wants with one's body. Fitted vests and T-shirts are worn to show off body adornment. Hoodies, once the staple wear for hip-hop gangster urban street fashion, are worn by sports people and celebrities of all nationalities. Designer brand, low-rise hanging jeans, showing off designer underwear, are popular with the young followers of street fashion.

During this period, I was a producer of stage plays, award ceremonies, documentaries and events. My experiences in the fashion industry came in useful. As a designer, the ability to predict fashion trends not only applied to designing clothes but covered a lifespan of arts and culture. The Art Foundation Course at Derby Art College back in the 1970s was the grounding for this, giving me the opportunity to experiment with different artistic mediums, and working in different creative industries. Working in commercial design at Davies and Field and the Lapaz shops was instrumental in the disciplines of forecasting and business leadership.

From experience in the retail business, I secured sponsorship from Hobbs, the ladies fashion company, for the actors' wardrobe for the *Living Under One Roof* stage play (2003 to 2007) until the final performance of the play at the Theatre Royal in Nottingham. I had written, directed and produced *Living Under One Roof* about a group of Caribbean migrants living in a house in Nottingham and the trials and tribulations that came with communal living.

The play (set in the early 1960s) and Hobbs had a distinct 1960s fashion signature. The garments acquired were woollen hobble skirts, colourful twin sets and the classic raincoats. We sourced vintage men's clothes for the lead actors: felt hats, mohair suits and fitted, long-sleeve (1960s) polo-style sweaters. The makeup company Mac sponsored the make-up for the cast.

By 2018, Caribbean men and women have adopted an even more personal 'lifestyle' approach to dress. This is due to the variety and choice of garments available in the shops and online shopping. We dress according to our immediate circumstances, how it fits in with our work, with our studies, our travel, how we socialise and how much is in our budget. We are the stylist; we coordinate what's available and, in many ways, help designers to create their collections. Inspiration now, more than ever, comes from diverse British communities.

Our three sons grew up watching and participating in this journey. As well as Warren being a successful illustrator in the film industry, Julian, our middle son, is a successful West End events producer and Miles is a photographer and editor-in-chief for *Fault Magazine*. Errol and I valued our university education and encouraged and supported our three sons to do the same. We both feel that proper grounding and family support is what young black people need to help them through the further education system.

When asked to be a board member of Nottingham Trent University, and the New Art Exchange in Nottingham, my immediate thought was about giving back to the community that had helped me so immensely.

Reflecting back to 2003 when I formed Tuareg Productions, people were talking about the Windrush Era, 1948 to 1962. If ever there was a conversation about coming to England, people would automatically refer to coming on a ship, and it became acceptable to assume all Caribbean people arrived by passenger liner cruise ship. The iconic black and white photographs and film clips of Caribbean men arriving at Tilbury Docks made an impact and are evidence of a migrant's journey. Sadly, there are hardly any images and press coverage of Caribbean people arriving via aeroplane at Gatwick in the 1950s and 1960s.

I do, however, remember my journey to Britain and value the importance of visual imagery. Therefore, I choose to present my story as a photographic journal of Caribbean family and business archives, signposted with contemporary illustrations.

The photographs chosen are unique and essential to the narratives of our everyday life – our stories amplified in what we wear, how we wear it and how we share information with future generations. The passing down of knowledge is paramount, and when the London Metropolitan Archives (LMA) asked me in 2015 to donate my designs and business archives, I was more than happy to oblige.

Style in my DNA is above all my journey as a black woman, wife, mother, fashion designer and businesswoman in 'making it happen' as a migrant in 21st-century Britain.

▲ Early 2000s London – bridal dress designed and made for Japanese client. © Tuareg Productions
▶ 2000 Nottingham – groom's outfit fashion statement: vivid blue frock coat. © Kenneth Harris

▲ 2000 Nottingham – bride and groom; Nottingham backdrop industrial landscape. © Kenneth Harris
▶ 2002 London – Black Film TV Awards. © Tuareg Productions

▲ 2004 London – British Caribbean youths hanging out; designer brand tracksuits and trainers. © Tuareg Productions

◄ 2003 London – formed Tuareg Productions; office wear. Photographer Damian Walker © Tuareg Productions

▲ 2006 Nottingham – *Living Under One Roof* stage production with Rachael Young and Samantha McDonald. Photographer Damian Walker © Tuareg Productions

◀ 2006 Nottingham – *Living Under One Roof* stage production at Theatre Royal Nottingham with Cathy Tyson. Photographer Damian Walker © Tuareg Productions

▲ 2006 London – British Museum: guests and performers at launch of *The Ones We Left Behind* stage production.
Photographer Damian Walker © Tuareg Productions

▶ 2006 London – British Museum; Hobbs silk chiffon dress and short cardigan with pearls.
Photographer Damian Walker © Tuareg Productions

THE
ONES
WE LEFT
BEHIND

▲ 2011 London – IWM Hanging Out; Images of Protest Forum. Photographer Damian Walker © Tuareg Productions
◀ 2000s London – African influences. Photographer Carol Williams © Tuareg Productions

OLYMPUS
HAS FALLEN
THEZONE
@
ROSEBANK
GREAT MOMENTS AT
THEIR GREATEST

▲ 2012 London – Hanging Out launch at the V&A. Photographer Damian Walker © Tuareg Productions
◀ 2012 Johannesburg, South Africa – film premier. © Tuareg Productions

▲ 2012 London – Hanging Out launch at the V&A; different looks. Photographer Damian Walker © Tuareg Productions

▶ 2012 London – Jamaica Hidden Histories project launch, at Jamaican High Commission. Photographer Damian Walker © Tuareg Productions

▲ 2014 London – family get together in high-profile location. Photographer Damian Walker © Tuareg Productions
◀ 2014 London – two generations, two styles. © Carol Williams

▲ 2014 London – socialising in high-profile venue. Photographer Damian Walker © Tuareg Productions

► 2015 London – Jamaica Hidden Histories exhibition gallery @ OXO; toned bodies.
Photographer Errol Holder © Tuareg Productions

ROOT

▲ 2015 London – Jamaica Hidden Histories exhibition gallery @ OXO.
Photographer Daniel McLeod © Tuareg Productions

▶ 2015 Nottingham – gala dinner: diverse communities. Photographer Keith O'Connor © Vida Harris

▲ 2015 – Mum celebrating her 80th birthday. Photographer Keith O'Connor © Vida Harris
▶ 2016 London – two generations; gala dinner. Photographer Errol Holder © Tuareg Productions

▲ 2000s London – making it happen. Photographer Miles Holder © Tuareg Productions